INK MONKEY

Also by Diana Hartog

Poetry

Matinee Light
Candy From Strangers
Polite To Bees

Fiction

The Photographer's Sweethearts

INK MONKEY

POEMS

Diana Hartog

Brick Books

Library and Archives Canada Cataloguing in Publication

Hartog, Diana
          Ink monkey : poems / Diana Hartog.

Poems.
ISBN 1-894078-50-0

          I. Title.

PS8565.A67155 2006   C811'.54   C2005-906802-7

We acknowledge the Canada Council for the Arts, the Government
of Canada through the Book Publishing Industry Development
Program (BPIDP), and the Ontario Arts Council for their support
of our publishing program.

Cover art: from Guérard, Henri-Charles. Sheet of 15 menus. Actual
size 16.5 by 21.5 cm. 19th cent. [etching]. Courtesy of the S.P. Avery
Collection, Miriam and Ira D. Wallach Division of Art, Prints and
Photographs, The New York Public Library, Astor, Lenox and Tilden
Foundations.

The author photograph is by Michael Hartog.

The book is set in Minion and Herculanum.

Design and layout by Alan Siu.

Printed and bound by Sunville Printco Inc.

Brick Books
431 Boler Road, Box 20081
London, Ontario N6K 4G6

brick.books@sympatico.ca

For Haven and Phoebe

Contents

∨ JAPANESE PRINTS

1

TWICE

Supposedly love, by Basho's day, could be mentioned only once in a series of linked poems, a rule often broken in Basho's school of poetics: Love could be mentioned twice.

Sleeves

Something "up his sleeve," as when a man in the West simply
leans against a wall with his hands in his pockets

and a woman walks by, her starched French cuff dangling an
abalone button blinded with thread. The Muse leaning also,

towards the East and the past: the poetic looseness of kimono sleeves,
damp with tears, in the Japanese canon of love. Sweet partings, trysts,

exposing always the wrist, its pale throat, the heartbeat's
muted throb at the fork of the two blue rivers

in that country.
     I have visited. Water lapped near, against

warm granite where we lay, sleeved in bodies, in their shudder
as the wind, almost dry, lifted us: thin material.

Cup

Tears serve a woman less as weapon
than a means to cup pain, and hand him the cup—to quaff
before he goes.

No use counting on the bars of black shadow
—pressed by the blinds
across his shoulders and arms
as he stands there by the door—
to bend less than she has to his body.

When a man is moved,
he will sometimes sit terribly still
and look away. No, he isn't thirsty.

Hieroglyphics

Plumed as the ostrich fan of an Egyptian underling
slowly spanning the hypotenuse between her mistress
and desire

the rushes bow
and lift: papyrus, bleached as the shaggy cough
of a lion taut at a leash and trembling. For who,

holding aloft the blue cloisonné jar crackled with copper
(so to speak of the sky), has broken it across his knee,
if not

he who parts the rushes, twisting a path between bluffs
pleated by erosion and bruised
purple at their base with the only shade? As the woman following,

I have learned to turn sideways, exposing
a single eye but both shoulders
towards the story.   Up ahead, scratched into stone,

he halts, his muscled torso latticed black, shadowed
with the reeds' wavering indifference;
reddish clay beds the stream, narrowed by thirst: "This is fine."

We lie down. Egypt covers us.
By my turned cheek
the water flexes clear, unaware of being the Nile.

The Mother Inside

Forgive me, that I've neglected you so long,
I was busy
writing down my sorrows.

Ah, and I too was alone
re-arranging some scraps of paper

This lake a thousand miles from a mother
stooped and in pain, as her vertebrae fail....
Among the pebbles, water laps softly.

These withered breasts
tingle with milk for you

His father had died, and oh! how I wrestled with that boy in
the flowering meadow, the imprint of our bodies—matted grass
and daisies—left behind as we hastened back to the wake.

Why do you always pick
these quarrels with love?

11

OASIS

Things get lost in the desert. —Even long naps, one afternoon to the next. A hat should always be worn against the sun.

To cope with the vast black sky, one can enroll in a class on Astronomy on Wednesday nights.

The class holds a "star party" at the top of a peak. It's cold, and windy. From the vans and station wagons the telescopes are unloaded— fat-barrelled, or slim and long and elegant. Everyone has their favourite constellations, ones they feel close to....

Oasis

The sound of each other, rustling,
the easy exchange through the air of insects and birds.

Noon, and to the south,
mercury shimmers in the wind-tousled palms—clustered to an oasis
when all else scatters sparse, flat, until troubled into mountains.

Near, the palms loom as mammoths, skirted with brown
down-drooping layers of years vulnerable to a
dropped match; a stray spark catching the imagination
where a trunk issues blackened and shorn.

In the hallowed clearing—palms towering in a shaggy ring—
recurs the wedding of place and time, attended by a sand-beetle
and mourned by the wind, which foresees with a rustle of taffeta
the early death of the bride.

       With evening,
what has died is the wind.

On the bluff, every creosote bush has gathered to a nucleus
its quail for the night: all one can safely know. The birds doze
in circles facing out—ready to scatter in overlapping rings at
the slightest mention.

Drifting, the high moon keeps its distance, holds it close
as I would be held.
       Let me guess: in a pool
half-hidden by reeds floats another moon—gilded, tremulous
from the glide of a water-strider. Am I close?
Am I even warm?

Creation, 3:30 pm, the Fifth Day

A lynx prowls past in the shade of the porch, tufted ears pricked to the silence; followed by her mate, the two tracking paw-prints like walking fists across the sand as they climbed the dune and disappear into the tamarisk on their rounds of the animal kingdom.

I must not be here yet.

The Seventh Day

In the shimmering heat every plant grows jealous
of its dime of shade, the coyotes slinking
backwards, all needs shrunken and
withdrawn into the brainstem

—though at dawn, the sharp spine of a cactus will attract
a single drop of dew and roll the tear down into the eye.

Forty days, we are told, and forty nights, Christ
consumed only his hunger, and poured
cool thirst over his hunched shoulders
as he sat, studying the palm of the human hand.

Certain Knowledge

Grain by grain, and gaining momentum with a shudder of sand down its flank, the white dune inches south, wormy with lizards. From the cool, loose interior the reptiles slither fringe-toed to the surface and air. Here they arch their necks, flood with warmth, and pursue the single blank thought of their species, the two beads of mercury unblinking. The creature holds still, perfectly still

as I climb; and stoop
for a wizened leather glove: petite, the two eyes
unbuttoned at the wrist.

Nightclass

The Mad Professor shouts, taps the blackboard with a stick
and paces to explain the great mating and uncoupling
of the planets: the retrograde dance, the southern reeling
of those ideas known as stars.

He cranks the system by hand
and the painted tin globes of Mercury & Venus & Mars
    —stiff-armed on wires—
revolve by jerks around a Sun with the rind of a grapefruit,
the sundry moons (some as tiny as peas) racing dizzily,

as the homeless of an L.A. alley lie stretched full-length
on broken sofas in the street: smoking, gazing up through a blur
of smog, at the flickering light of past mistakes
they can now pinpoint.

The Moon and Firestone

Let's take a look at the moon as a beautiful woman—half angry,
half full. Ringed with industry's sanguine fumes she rises
above the Hollywood Freeway, Friday midnight, clots of traffic
moving sluggishly if at all, the cars' occupants
audience to this B-Grade movie, an old one with Bette Davis
ascending the staircase in a close-up; the atmosphere
exaggerating every pore of a landscape cratered with hurled rocks,

while privately,
beneath the overpass, the heavy *thud* of someone's heart
is let drop to the sidewalk in a brown paper bag.

Though the city has limits: a stutter of lights, virgin
culs-de-sac, half-acre lots yet to be sold where a cloverleaf
juts into unfinished space; the cured concrete dangles steel
reinforcement above a man hurrying home at dawn, clutching
a new Sunbeam toaster, the cut on his hand bleeding

as fields of strawberries and the bent knuckled spines
of migrants in flowered shirts flash by,
harvested in turn by desert, where armies of windmills
flail the Santa Ana winds
and billboards of waving neon fronds solicit at every exit
as the highway eases from pavement to gravel to dirt, to a trail
freshened by coyotes trotting north to the next oasis in search of
fallen dates in this Garden.

Settling for Palm Springs,
the white morning moon
allows the mundane purchase of four steel-belted radials
to eclipse her briefly—their mounting and balancing—
as she drifts, wan and obscure, above the dealership;
a moon snubbed with cigarette butts; smudged; erased;
a sphere rounded-off to the last digit of the national debt,

yet still she comes around,
drawn, presumably, by what she sees in
this desert of wrecking yards, trailer courts, canyons filled with tires;
a satellite lured into orbit
around our crusted metallic core; as if we were interesting,
and might change.

Glass

Lurched from sleep by an earthquake
I grope for the switch—the gooseneck lamp
bent low
as if to drink from the glass of trembling water.

I see that sand has drifted in across the night,
which explains my dream, of a meteorite
hurtling through webbed glass
to land softly on my stomach: still smoking yet strangely cold
and the size of a scorched orange.

I smooth the coverlet, inspect a tiny cigarette burn.
That worn bullet-hole in the windowpane
will have to be stopped.

The Link between Reader and Writer

Perhaps you're sitting up in bed, and have tilted
the light to the page so as not to disturb lying beside you
another person.

Or listening for the children's squeals from the
upstairs tub, you have gone to kneel
and with a towel blot their sturdy little bodies

—leaving this face down on the couch.

Outside in the random silence, the desert wind
is jangling against the flagpole
some metal thing.

Dust Devils

Dark clouds hurry toward the end of the world,
mesquite shivers,
winds swirl at random—vortices
of sand and dust caught-up-with-the-devil
          up folds of erosion.

Mourners high on the ridge, heads bowed
to the pure of heart,
forgive the Priest's discreet pleasure in mouthing *"Ashes to ashes…"*
     —gusts twist the hem of his cassock—

forgive his white socks.

Ultraviolet

Black widows crawl up under the skirts
of the *Washingtonia filifera*,
and a sidewinder
wraps its chill length around the warmth of a boulder
        (the way the mind
                    coils around its brain)
and drops off to sleep.

For those who can't
sleep,
a glass tube of light—ultraviolet, waved like a wand, low to the sand—
divines the white-blue glow of scorpions
burrowed in hibernation, buffered
against the glittering stars, against the cold idea

of Scorpio: slowly revolving, stinger arched.

Entry

The silence of the desert is too strong for the walls of the ranch house. The feeble bleats of the radio are overpowered at night by the presence of the high white dune to the west, by the whispers of the tamarisk around a hidden, needle-strewn grave.

And even in here I can feel the stars through the ceiling; feel their glitter at the roof of my skull as each new spark of thought is snuffed; overwhelmed by an intelligence which thinks not in words but in Bears, Scorpions, Giants with fine diamond-edged swords. And sapphire-set Dippers—bent at the handle to scoop the mercury of memory, or whatever it is, off the top of our heads, that gods drink.

Meridian

Water trickles into the ear: a stream snaking across the oasis.
Bees drone high in the medulla.
The yellowing cottonwood flowers with a sweet humming—consumed
when the swarm departs from the silenced limbs.

The silent Rudolph Valentino in *Son of the Sheik*
slipped his hand to the small of a starlet's back
and bent her to the-kiss-of-all-time under these palms,
the klieg lights
shining far brighter

than this moon—pale and wafer-thin,
fragile against the blue;
for daylight
has again undone the moon

as we are all undone—the starlet lifting her arms, stretching.
We who have gravity to blame for how far
we fall, how soon
warm sand
slips through the narrow glass waist of the hour.

Mirage

*There's even a rusty sip left
in the tin cup.*

Around the shallow green pool
fan-palms tower.   A cottonwood leans.
Reeds bend low over the bank's soft lip, where the real
and the reflected
drink from the same source.

Birds of the oasis divide their time between the two
　　—as they dip and swerve and flit
　　　　from branch,
　　　　　　to reflected branch

III

FALSE START

A tiny monkey weighing just 200 grams and thought to be extinct has been rediscovered in south-eastern China, reports The People's Daily. *The "ink" or "pen" monkeys were once kept by scholars to prepare ink, pass brushes and turn pages; the highly intelligent creatures, who slept in desk drawers or brush pots, evidently added to a scholar's reputation for eccentricity.*

Ink Monkey

He's a great help.

While I stretch
he grinds the ink-stick in the shallow well: the rhythmic
                        shuuss…shuuss…shuuss…
soothes.   He spits again. *Shuuss…*
*shuuss…*the liquid darkening.

A strange hunched creature, trembling at every task.
He can't write. Not poetry.
Oh, he can wield a brush
and stroke a character
                 —even a string of characters—
rewarding himself with a raisin for every page
turned.   Scribble scribble.
Scribble scribble scribble.   Off in his own world.

Ignored (the best lot for a poet), and fresh from a nap in
the upper left-hand drawer,
I forget everything I've been taught
—cooling my tiny brain—

and begin:
dip my tail—just the tip—
into the ink.

Frog Contest

False start:
false fronts, saloons, wooden sidewalks,
the crowd booing
             as the green contestant is
         carried back to
the line drawn in the dust

❧

Playing leap-frog
the small boy crouches,
tailbone tucked

❧

Mention of a dragon in Japanese linked-verse
is limited to
"once every thousand stanzas."
No restrictions on frogs

❧

Freed by a kiss
he lowers himself into the cool muck

❧

While applause swells for the hypnotist, the bullfrog
leaps from the stage
to regain his seat in the second row
where, warts and all, he sinks down
and reaches for his wife's hand

❧

Hind legs dangling, the old poet
treads water, obscure among the reeds.
Famous pond

The Couple in Room 12

Swans-down in the ashtray. Pillows flung to the floor.
Thank Jupiter for maid service.
No need to pick up after him
in here,
or in the bathroom—where he treads damp towels
                              and hisses in the steam.

The TV flickering mute, its remote
knocked to the carpet
by a wing.

Leda, sprawled across the sheets, naked,
—mind a blank—
stares up at the ceiling's watermarks.   Slowly turns her head
towards the high window   and the plucked moon
                              above the motel.

IV

JELLYFISH SUITE

A single jellyfish battered by winter waves can sometimes be found stranded on the shore, a gelatinous blur: blue—a brilliant blue mandala; or black— a melted tire. White scraps of paper, hundreds of tiny scraps like the notes we write to ourselves but erased and drying in tatters among the pebbles: that's what remains when a swarm of moon jellies is dragged in, caught in a tide.

Otherwise there's the Aquarium to visit.

—Or the mind's eye, in which the infamous Portuguese man-of-war glistens near-invisible, adrift on the surface tension while dangling, fathoms down, a hidden agenda of stinging cells, difficult for a swimmer to see in the greenish mote-hung gloom. The striated iris; the pupil, the way it appears to dilate, expansive, or contract from glare, from the pointed question: the eye shares so much with the jellyfish. Both so tender, so innocent and ephemeral, shrinking from touch; and their beauty, from comprehension.

Chrysaora, or "Sea Nettle"

The sting of beauty
loosens the muscles that hinge the jaw,
tongue slack, saliva pooling

as the eye
      follows the ascension of sheer being
          —veil over mystery over veil,
               frilly mouth-arms trolling, tentacles streaming—

while all attempts
fail,
all attempts by the tongue…

before the jellyfish
leaves the scene, wholly innocent, yet
deadly as love-at-first-sight;

and only human, you might—but don't—
take it personally.

"Egg-Yolk" Jelly

So named
for the morning after a quarrel, rising exhausted
to the nothing
left from nothing-left-unsaid;

transparent as the matter in
What's the matter?

or merely the day's first sputum
afloat in the basin—drifting, aimless—

surely what the brain loses when it loses its mind,
this listless blur that randomly

gathers to a pang   a semblance   for one pulse…two…even three

before it dies away
so tattered and diaphanous

you'd never guess.

Pleurobrachia, or "Sea Gooseberry"

—drifting in the current,
a tiny light-bulb of feeble
wattage flickering along loops of filament,

small as the bulb of a penlight travelling
in the dark of a woman's purse

the way I travelled inside my mother before her water broke,
buoying her fears; lids closed over bulbous eyes

only to blink
in the glare, squinting as I lay in her freckled arms
against a hospital gown smelling of bleach.

Each of us gasping for breath.

You're so little, and know so little
beyond instinct, you assume—with a feeble, flickering brilliance—
that you've both washed ashore
together;
assume she's holding you like this, so tight, because
little as you are, you've saved her,   your mother.

Quince Jelly

It's the thinnest of skins, the membrane between
being and nothingness: transparent,
or opaque

—or sometimes both, as when sealing a row of half-pint jars,
the clear melted paraffin
clouding as it cools and slowly hardening
towards the centre—still soft,
                              you could poke a finger;

the jelly trembling when disturbed
and such a beautiful colour, an ethereal amber but pale,
pale and translucent,
the colour, say,
of the soul

freshly entered through the top
of the infant's skull,
the soft fontanel finally closing
to the light streaming down
as the bones knit together: *That will have to do.*

A jellyfish is not a fish; it has no lungs, heart, muscles, bones. Simple neurons help it move, with sensors around the rim detecting up from down, light from dark.

A Moon Jelly

Rare—since they commonly drift in swarms—
to view a lone
moon jelly

the whitish-opaque bell
doubly veiled: picture

a light mist across
a moon
seen through eyes
clouded; one's thoughts elsewhere

Notes to the Composer:

What I'd like is a suite comprised of 97% water (as are jellyfish), to be conducted at night, outside, with fireflies blinking and stars. Those in attendance will lie on their backs on the damp grass. A simple moon jelly will float past, with a pulse like that of a heart, the way it can skip a beat, or three, or four—a drifting silence in the chest.

That's what we expect from the sea: deep down, we expect silence. In the Midwater's permanent night, galaxies of *noctiluca* wink bioluminescent. After-images, plucked blindly and at random. ...Strings. Timpani. Notes faint but gathering strength in numbers—in the hundreds, even thousands. Muted horns coming up for air beneath a swarm of moon jellies pulsing willy-nilly, feeding on scum among anchored yachts.

I can send along a guidebook—*The Common Gelatinous Animals*—filled with the lyricals of genus and species: *Aurelia labiata, Pelagia colorata, Velella velella.* (Velella velella!) The diagrams point to body parts as to parts of speech when plumbing the mystery of a simple sentence: oral groove, wing plate, tentacle, gill, keel, velum, comb row— to name a few.

The mind descends as in a diving bell. An undulating wisp of neon tickertape: *Cestum veneris.* A sparkling fishing net flung out without further thought: *Praya dubia.* ("*Dubia*" is Latin for doubtful.)

In a tiny silver box I've kept what's left of a jellyfish, dried up, a few grains of sand. I lift the lid, and look at it. The human brain, as it seeks to comprehend, is comprised of only 80% water. *There's a moment in a jelly's slow forward pulse when its wake hangs suspended—jellyfish-shaped, a play-on-water exact enough for a turtle to snap at—before it dissolves....*

Yes, there are dangers (the sting of the tiny Australian sea wasp, *Chironex*, can kill within minutes), but aren't they everywhere? —And jellyfish, with their thin skin, and even when in their element, are prey to more than most. (They seem to *invite* metaphor.)

The play of tenderness across a lover's face: that's how ephemeral they are. A jelly will sense an observer, sense undue interest; even *fond* can be too strong a word. And a wave can tear them to shreds.

That's why I thought, *music.* Sharps and flats on paper, but in the air, floating, what harm?

Symbiosis

Brief flashes of intelligence
glimpsed
among trolling white billows of oral arms
                       as *Drymonema* drifts oblivious

are tiny fish
that flit quicksilver
nibble leftovers
avoid
the long whipping tentacles strung with stinging cells
dart
as memory darts

Little Jerks

The erratic young
—moon jellies in miniature, countless air-bubbles, fringed—
contract in sneezes *ah-choo* *ah-choo* as they pulse in frantic
jerks past full-blown *Aurelia labiata* and sometimes get in
the way: Bump
the scalloped hem

of a bell that's begun to expand in vol-
                uptuous slow motion … …*Ah*—… … …*Ah*—…

Hot

Twisted from the socket
Aglantha is set adrift on the alternating current.
                              Coiled live wires
dangle in the jelly's wake: sprung curls
that glow a shocking party-orange; the name "*Aglantha*"

like a backward glance
inviting the tongue to repeat,   *Hot!…Aglantha*—the Greek ("Glorious
Bloom") seductive
music whispered in his ear, the party
elsewhere, *Goodnight, be good, go to sleep,*
don't touch

The Psychoanalysis of Dreams

Every night, millions of jellyfish pulse to the surface of the world's
oceans to feed; a great migration from the depths,
a vast exhalation of images sheer and
amenable, they could mean anything—

    ghostly parachutes, dangling empty harnesses as they rise,
    "mushroom" spores drifting up in all innocence from the cloud,
    white blood cells swarming to a wound

—but nearer the surface and four in the morning, lying
awake, we see them for what they are: recurrent dreams
on their way to tomorrow night

except for a few stragglers and hangers-on; the stray apparition,
tardy, confused;

the dead son—a helicopter gunner in Vietnam—who appears
    at the foot of the bed
in the wrong room
the wrong house,
the neighbour crying out in her sleep, sitting up, *No, dear,*
next door! —*Your mother will be so happy!*

Jellyfish Costume

You will need

        a clear plastic umbrella
        narrow scarlet ribbons
        several pink feather-boas

and a child, to grip the umbrella's handle under the clear plastic bell. Tie a cape of feathery pink mouth-arms around his neck: these to gather and filter any treats. At each spoke of the open umbrella, attach the long narrow ribbons to curtain him in stinging red tentacles, before he ventures out beyond the gate and its jingling bell. —Caught up in the early dark, drifting with the current of sodden ghosts and pirates and bumblebees along the sidewalk in the rain.

The Moon Jelly Room

Waves continue to arc in great swells and break
thunderous along the shore of Monterey Bay

while sheltered from wind and rain we shuffle
through the narrow *Moon Jelly Room*—mirrored at either end to reflect
the crowd into infinity: cameras, perambulators, the smell of wet wool.

moon jellies moon jellies　　—A current of saltwater
pumped from the Aquarium basement buoys them either side
behind floor-to-ceiling glass.　*moon jellies moon jellies*

Pulsing at either temple, they belie the variety
of plaid, striped, flowered and black umbrellas snapped violently
inside-out, spokes broken:

these fringed white
parasols floating up in a watery blue sky.　Myriad, they pulse,
        and drift like happy memories

for anyone to recall, anyone
in this mirrored crowd: awed there could be so many,
and so alike, as if all happy memories were alike.

The Deep Blue

"Spots excite me"—Miró

In playful old age
the great artist doodled jellyfish—
a circle here, some wavy lines there, ta-*dah!*
—after his afternoon nap.

An old man's nap; long, fitful.　　Waking
only to sink back.　　Saliva
drooling on the pillow
to form

a damp spot the subconscious
can't resist—adding a fringe of tentacles
　　　　　　drawn out of the deep blue
　　　　　　with a brush of a single hair.

V

JAPANESE PRINTS

Typical of the imagination is to leap ahead, conjure the future scene by scene, out-of-sequence perhaps, as the mind wanders among fears and hopes. In the literary tradition of Japan this eagerness finds solace in the Farewell Poem. Meant as one's penultimate poem, to be intoned on the eve of one's death, a summation, it is often carried about for years in the head of the poet. Rolled upon the tongue as it undergoes interminable revision— even while the poet enjoys rude health as he travels along the road chosen.

The Tokaido Road—or rather, The Fifty-three Stages of the Tokaido, a series of woodblock prints by the master 19th century artist, Utagawa Hiroshige—travels in the imagination along the eastern sea route leading from Edo to the imperial capital at Kyoto. Hiroshige himself took liberties: he was known to shift a mountain for artistic purposes, and even weightier, a season; all the while harbouring a deep respect for nature's continuity.

The series of fifty-five colour prints—landscapes, one for each relay station along the Tokaido and one each for the terminal points—covers a distance of some three hundred miles. In numerical progression, Station seven, of course, follows Station six; and forty-six, forty-five. Contrary to that law, but in the spirit of dreams "roaming over a wild moor," the following poems are presented in the sequence in which they were written, day after day; best not to switch them around, stir up dust.

That image of you: your bald and noble head turning for a last glimpse of the known.

Perhaps you have passed the scene on this postcard. Is it much changed? Already you'll be gathering to memory: pines, wind, the steep mountain road, to keep all that passes fresh. Brush and ink and straw raincoat—these you took, but left behind your battered travel diary. Read, and re-read; the hours moving slowly, steadily.

(A detour forced a crossing
        high above mist and fissured boulders
        suspended cliff to cliff, the sagging reed footbridge
                alive to our every step.

Resolved by Shig,
my young companion on this journey: To cut from his death poem
                all clutter.)

Station 37—Akasaka

Inn at Akasaka

...Ah! The man on his way to Edo last month
has returned, on his way home: the fingers of the blind masseur
follow a scar, familiar,
across thick shoulders damp from the baths.

Station 16—Kambara

Village, Night, Winter

Apparent strangers trudge in opposite directions
to balance a composition,
figures in a landscape,

passing; each back hunched
under a separate burden of snowflakes—falling even
as we speak.

According to legend, a pregnant woman from Nissaka set out after dark for Kanaya to see her husband, but was attacked and killed by bandits. "Her blood fell on a large round boulder"—which now obstructs the path, and weeps every night in sorrow for her.

Station 26—Nissaka

The Night-Weeping Stone

Bow, fellow traveller, to the boulder
blocking our progress to the capital.

Bow, and be rebuked—as am I—
for a heart long hardened against stone.

Droplets slowly trickle down the rough cheek.

Night-mist, some will say, or *Early-morning dew*;
perhaps both

weep over the plight of the sole
witness to the horror: a boulder; mute;
one "not particularly distinctive or unusual."

Station 17—Yui

View of Mt. Fuji

Along the coast from Kambara we travelled, my companion twice pausing to repair his sandal. It rained. Then the sky cleared. We resisted even a brief glance back to gauge our progress, for fear of a view of Fuji premature to that from Satta Pass, highly prized. The road tireless under our feet as we climbed.

> That night spent
> at a lowly inn,
> the mountain's image
> clouded by fitful dreams   *Written by Shig*

High at Satta Pass, the view was as promised. Ancient pines clung to the verge and leaned out into eternity: I could do no less, my coat-tail clutched taut from behind in Shig's grip.

Station 18—Okitsu

Two Sumo Wrestlers Being Carried across a Shallow Stream

All in all
a light effort:

one wrestler sags the spine of a horse; the other

that of a palanquin, four bald porters in loincloths
struggling to shoulder the weight as they wade, ankle-deep;
the giant, pipe in hand, leans to one side, stretches his thick neck,
eyes the water.

The mountain called Fudesute—which means "to throw away the brush"—is named for the dramatic gesture of a great artist of the Muromachi period (1492–1573), when he encountered the mountain for the first time and despaired of ever capturing its beauty and strangeness.

Station 49—Sakanoshita

Tea Shop with View of Mt. Fudesute

The day's hundredth fly exits
a blank mind.

Blink, and the light shifts.

The tea served here is soon lukewarm
in the open air

and the waterfalls across the gorge
lend their mist.

Due to the mountain's reputation
no one else is attempting a sketch.

Station 46—Shono

Driving Rain at Shono

Tucked under a ledge, one can follow a single raindrop among
thousands in the long straight fall
to the gorge below: Summer rain.

In Autumn, inside, out of the rain, paging through a book of Japanese
prints we come upon *sheets* of rain slanted steeply and figures
                    hunched and stumbling at a run, pummelled.

The clash of strong, straight lines angled at cross-purposes like spears
provoked French artists to attempt Hiroshige's
Winter rain.

Spring rain returns with many light, delicate lines
slanted in harmony. —Some mist; nothing to it;
a few drips from the brim of one's hat.

Station 53—Kusatsu

The Shop at Kusatsu

Broiled clams, specialty of the port of Kuwana.
At Ishibe: that excellent bean curd coated with bean paste.
—Not forgetting the yam soup at Mariko....
And now for the famous rice cakes of Kusatsu.

A proprietor so often accused—unjustly!—of altering his recipe
by return customers.

Station 54—Otsu

Inn at Otsu

Taken ill
I regret, in clear-headed moments,
the too-short pause at Mishima
miles back.
One's eyes should not be closed against the greatness of the past
                                    even if hidden in mist.

Looking for the shrine
we might have become lost.

Shig, also, visited by pains in his stomach.

Yet one could have spared an hour;
what is an hour, when stolen from arrival?

In 1499 an earthquake and tidal wave washed away a narrow plug of land between Lake Hamana and the sea. Female travellers who are betrothed regard the ferry crossing at Imagiri (which means "now broken") as inauspicious for their marriage prospects.

Station 39—Okazaki

Imagiri: the Narrow Mouth of the Lake

Hymen broken, cherry blossoms in bloom, the new bride—preparing soba noodles the traditional way—muses happily: *I could have crossed at Imagiri, everything would have turned out the same.* Instead, she had walked between her superstitious mother and aunt, needless miles around the shore of the lake, in detour. No one alluding to the cataclysmic event.

Miles, with eyes downcast under wide hats.

Forest of a Thousand Pines

From the Forest of a Thousand Pines and its deep silence, I emerged at dusk, having followed the voices of children gathering cones into baskets.

There was still time: the darkening sea stretched far to the line of a horizon as yet unbroken by the special moon. The waters deceptively calm, as if this were any night. Against my better judgment I sought out the hut of a local poet. We had met once before, in Edo, but hold differing views. Finally the way was pointed through a maze of alleys.

I found him shivering but in high spirits, cowled in a blanket, revising his poems. —One of which, he claimed, is to be anthologized.

Worried about the moon, I soon left.

Station 54—Otsu

Otsu, Again, Lake Biwa

Among haze
ridges rising steeply along the shore
           echo one beyond the other

Up ahead, at Station 45, awaits a temple's statue of the Buddha Yakushi, carved from natural rock: a statue considered particularly effective as a guardian against adversity and attracting many worshippers.

Station 40—Chiryu

The beauty of the wild irises, alas,
cannot guard against misfortune.

Station 8—Hiratsuka

The Broad Plain

Another courier flies past, sandals flapping in the dust. One grows used to them, as they relay towards Edo. When from the distance a bare-chested man comes running towards me—headlong, as if robbed of his clothes and fleeing for his life—my heart continues to plod undisturbed.

Yet when footsteps pound from behind and draw close at my back—a young courier bound for Kyoto, breath coming in gasps as he scatters beads of sweat—my pace quickens: Again I'm to be overtaken!

I must learn from example.
A roadside pine.

Station 9—Oiso

The Rain of Tora

A grey day. Grey thoughts kept my eyes downcast to the muddy road, busy with footprints. Bones ache in such weather. In youth, my path solitary. But today I welcomed the mournful tale—that of a mother, Tora, and her fierce love for the child lost to her—which hovers above this village; and the chance to join my tears with the rain.... It was only a fleeting shower.

My companion expressed surprise.

I explained. —The passing of old parents. Ever-fresh, is a child's grief.

Fishing boats floated out on the bay soaked in sunshine.

Station 20—Fuchu

At Fuchu, no bridge yet spans the river. The scenery here has inspired many a traveller to declaim, impromptu, a few lines; sometimes midstream, when balanced on the shoulders of a porter as he fords the current, waist-deep.

> The Tokaido, long travel-worn
> stops short
> at the bank of the Abe River
>
> —and continues, refreshed,
> from the opposite shore.

Or sometimes in relief, when, having crossed, he is lowered to the sand, tabi dry.

Station 35—Yoshida

Repair of the Castle Roof

Like those workers, I, too, would
scurry up bamboo scaffolding
                    if afforded a view
                    of my fear

far below:
a speck
moved along the Toyokawa River.

Written by Shig

Kyoto

Nihombashi

Who can forget the thrust of departure from Edo—porters, horses,
pugs, palanquins—spilling over the bridge into the eye?

Nor can I now, at this late hour, mend the gaps in the Tokaido: when,
sunk in thought, I left others to tend the beauty of the fields.

Behind, at Chiryu,
the eight-fold bridge lies in ruins in the marsh, unseen.

Nor at Okabe were we beset by bandits! And
at Hokane Pass barrier-gate: I resent
being squeezed through a knothole by the government.

Of smells, only those pungent wafts from the horse market linger....
Birdsong may have floated at my ear for miles, unheard.

My companion cautions against such pangs. "The end and
the beginning continually pass each other like couriers at run
between two great cities, back and forth, at all points along the way."

To return to the crossing at Arai: I would again
look deeply into the countenance of the old ferryman who claimed
that of all possible human faces, there are only seven.

Station 51—Mizuguchi

Gourd-Drying

A pink yawn
from the infant
bound to his sister's back.
He tips forward
as she stoops.
Rears upright without complaint as she lifts another gourd.
Blinks. Eyes wide. Contemplates, over her shoulder,
the world, yet another view
—till wrenched away.

Acknowledgements

Some of these poems appeared previously in the following publications: *The Capilano Review*, *Brick: a literary journal*, *Gargoyle* [Virginia], *Northern Lights* [London, England]. The "Oasis" series was originally published in *The Malahat Review*, and then in *The New Long Poem Anthology*—from Coach House Books and now from Talon Books.

I am grateful to the Canada Council and to the B.C. Arts Council for their financial support; and for residency fellowships at The MacDowell Colony, The Virginia Center for the Creative Arts, and Hawthornden Castle International Retreat for Writers.

My thanks to the Powell family of Chimney Ranch for their generosity over the years, in letting me write in the Fort. And my thanks to David Badke, especially; always my "first reader." Thanks also to Katherine Westerhout for taking me to view the prints of Hiroshige and Hokusai; to Dan and Judy Phillips of Windsor Arms for sanctuary when I needed it; and to editor Marnie Parsons for her apt guidance.

*D*iana Hartog arrived in British Columbia with her family from San Francisco in 1970. She travels widely in the winter; otherwise she lives in New Denver and writes in a studio perched on the side of a mountain. She is the author of three previous collections of poetry and a novel.